DIGGING FOR TREASURE

Expository Preaching: Revelation Today!

Edited by
David A. Hull and John Wiltshire

A met Publication

Published on behalf of MET by

tel: 0115 932 0643 web: www.moorleys.co.uk

ISBN 978 0 86071 691 4

© Copyright 2014 MET

All rights reserved.
No part of this publication may be reproduced, stored in a retrieval system, or transmitted, in any form or by any means, electronic, mechanical, photocopying, recording or otherwise, without the prior written permission of the publishers.

British Library Cataloguing in Publication Data.
A catalogue record for this book is available from the British Library.

MOORLEYS
Print & Publishing
tel: 0115 932 0643 web: www.moorleys.co.uk

Contents

	Page
INTRODUCTION *David A. Hull*	1
EXPOSITORY PREACHING: REVELATION TODAY! *Peter C. Graves*	5
PREACHING APOCALYPTICS *Steve Brady*	25
THE REFRESHING WORK OF THE HOLY SPIRIT *Chris Blake*	45
CONCLUSION *John Wiltshire*	65

Methodist Evangelicals Together
is the largest independent organisation in British Methodism today, uniting and representing evangelicals at every level within our denomination.

Our three core purposes are:
- **ADVOCATING:** Promoting and representing evangelicalism within Methodism, and Wesleyan evangelicalism within the wider evangelical world.
- **EQUIPPING:** Providing resources through publications, conferences and our website for evangelicals within British Methodism.
- **SUPPORTING:** Offering pastoral support and advice to evangelicals, who can often feel isolated within Methodism and face particular pressures.

MET is a fellowship for every Methodist who shares our desire to:
- Uphold the authority of Scripture
- Seek Spiritual Renewal
- Pray for Revival
- Spread Scriptural holiness
- Emphasise the centrality of the Cross

MET promotes partnership in the Gospel to proclaim Jesus as Lord. Our partners include:
- Cliff College
- ECG
- Share Jesus International
- Inspire Network

Join MET and partner with us to:
- *Network with evangelical Methodists in prayer and action.*
- *Add your voice to over 2000 others on key issues at all levels of the Methodist Church and beyond.*
- *Participate in national and local events.*
- *Receive the MET Connexion Magazine.*

Find us at: www.methodistevangelicals.org.uk

or write to us
c/o Moorleys Print & Publishing, 23 Park Road, Ilkeston, Derbys DE7 5DA
who will pass on your valued enquiry.

INTRODUCTION
David A. Hull
Methodist Minister,
Yeovil & Blackmore Vale Circuit

Expository preaching depends absolutely upon a Christian understanding of 'revelation'. We seek, in our preaching, to expound the Bible because we believe it is the Word of God, through which God chooses to reveal himself today. In the opening words of the letter to the Hebrews, the author reminds us that, 'In the past God spoke to our forefathers through the prophets at many times and in various ways, but in these last days he has spoken to us by his Son' (Hebrews 1:1-2a). In the early Church, the first believers discovered that, as the Holy Spirit moved amongst them, that supreme revelation of God in Jesus was made known to them as they 'devoted themselves to the apostles' teaching' (Acts 2:42). The same is true today. As we devote ourselves to the teaching of the prophets in the Old Testament and the apostles in the New, God reveals himself to us in Jesus.

As preachers, we depend upon revelation in both our preparation and our proclamation, for we know that we can only understand the Bible ourselves as God reveals its truth to us and that our hearers will only receive and respond to the message if the Holy Spirit opens hearts and minds as we preach. Both preacher and congregation depend on the revelation of the Holy Spirit. When we proclaim what the Lord has revealed to us, we pray that our congregations will share in the experience of Lydia as she heard an apostle preach on a riverbank many years ago: 'The Lord opened her heart to respond to Paul's message' (Acts 16:14b).

Preaching must therefore be accompanied by fervent prayer, asking God to reveal himself in our preparation and through our proclamation. The renowned preacher of a former generation, Charles Haddon Spurgeon wrote, in *Lectures to my Students*, 'The preacher who neglects to pray much must be very careless about … ministry, cannot have comprehended [the] calling [and] cannot have computed the value of a soul, or estimated the meaning of eternity'. It has been well said that we should pray as though all depended on God and then prepare and preach as though all depended on our speaking and the response of our hearers.

In *Digging for Treasure: Revelation Today*, we focus, therefore, on this central place of revelation in the task of expository preaching. In the opening chapter, Peter Graves maintains that there is still a central place for preaching in today's Church and argues that one of the greatest needs within the Church is for preaching which *teaches*. He shows how expository preaching can fulfil this role as it seeks both to take seriously and open up the Biblical text whilst also addressing modern-day issues with contemporary application. He explores how preachers can be authentic in their preaching, effective in their communication and offers guidelines for the preparation of sermons which, in delivery, will help the congregation to encounter the living Lord who reveals himself through the written and proclaimed Word.

Continuing the theme of revelation, we turn in the second chapter to consider the Book of Revelation, also known as 'The Apocalypse'. It is a book that preachers have found to be notoriously difficult to expound, but Steve Brady encourages us to work hard at seeking to understand all that the book has to teach us, for hard work will be greatly rewarded. He identifies the book's genre, reviews the differences in interpretation that have emerged over the years and offers a case study, demonstrating how principles of interpretation should be applied. He shows clearly that the book of Revelation continues to be relevant today and encourages us never to lose sight of its main purpose: to help us to see Jesus, for he is the one who is ultimately revealed through every page of the book, as throughout the whole Bible.

Revelation, in its broadest sense, is in the end attainable, not by human effort, but only by the work of the Holy Spirit. That is why we have included, as our third chapter, a sermon preached by Chris Blake as part of the MET Celebration held at the Methodist Conference in 2014. He reminds us that the work of the Spirit is indispensable in the life of the Church, that the refreshing power of the Holy Spirit is daily available to us and that it is for all, for transformation and for mission.

That brings us back to our theme, 'revelation', for as we reach out in mission and as we seek to expound the Bible from the pulpit, people will only respond as their hearts are opened by the Lord in the power of the Holy Spirit. The role of the Spirit and God's work of revelation come together in the first prayer found in the letter to the Ephesians. Clearly the apostle, Paul wanted to encourage the Christians to whom he was writing and he knew that what would encourage them most was greater revelation: that the curtains would be drawn back, that their eyes would be opened and that they would be able to see more clearly who God is, all that he has done for them and the hope that he brings. Surely a similar prayer should be in our hearts as we prepare to preach and as we proclaim the Word of God in our own day:

> I keep asking that the God of our Lord Jesus Christ, the glorious Father, may give you the Spirit of wisdom and revelation so that you may know him better. I pray also that the eyes of your heart may be enlightened in order that you may know the hope to which he has called you ... (Ephesians 1:17-18a)

EXPOSITORY PREACHING: REVELATION TODAY!

Peter C. Graves
Supernumerary Methodist Minister

It was a special service, so the Bishop came to preach. As the people left, many complimented him on the sermon, but one shabby man looked him straight in the eye and mumbled 'Pathetic'. Later he came back and said 'Very, very boring'. Afterwards the Bishop asked the Rector, 'Who was that strange man?' 'Oh don't worry about him,' said the Rector, 'he's a bit simple, and just wanders around repeating what he hears others saying'.

Unfortunately, preaching does not get a good press these days. All too often, sermons lack vitality and energy and are viewed as dull, boring and irrelevant. Although the message may be true, many feel that they've heard it all before, so it has become stale. Consequently they approach it with no sense of expectancy, and only listen out of courtesy. Not surprisingly therefore, many of our people complain that they are not being fed in worship. There are, of course, exceptions to every rule, but most of us are aware of the need for better preaching, and for it to be both life-related and thoroughly Biblical.

Hence this publication. We are seeking to explore Expository Preaching with a special emphasis on 'Revelation Today'. We want to explore how we can share the revealed truth of scripture so that it makes sense today and comes alive in the hearts and minds of our hearers.

Bernard Manning defined preaching as 'a manifestation of the incarnate word, from the written word, by the spoken word'[1]. As preachers, therefore, we must take the Bible seriously. It is our calling to explore in some depth the message of God, which has been revealed in scripture, and supremely in the life, death and resurrection of Jesus Christ. Then with the help of the Holy Spirit we pray that our hearers will encounter the living Christ and experience his transforming power. We long to help our congregations discover the reality and relevance of a living faith. We still believe in the efficacy of preaching. We want to become better at it and wish to develop our skills and increase our understanding of the craft.

Back in the year 2000, in an article entitled 'Preaching, Theology, and Spirituality in Twentieth Century British Methodism', Methodist Minister John Munsey Turner reflected on the need for a rediscovery of the importance of preaching in Methodism. He wrote:

> When I became a tutor at Queen's College, Birmingham in 1970, preaching in its traditional form seemed in eclipse. Educationalists scorned it, oratory was at a discount, the authority figure was suspect, there were plenty of alternatives to the sheer slog of the craft and art of sermon making, but not the slightest evidence that they attracted people to the churches. By 1975 students actually wanted to learn the craft. The grumble now is at the lack of role models.[2]

It is, of course, true that times have changed and that, in the television age, the era of great oratory has come to an end. It certainly does no good to hanker after the successes of a

---

[1] Quoted in Quicke, Michael *360 Degree Preaching* (Grand Rapids, Michigan: Baker Academic, 2003) p. 26
[2] Turner, J. M. *The Expository Times* (January 2000) p. 116

time long since passed. Nevertheless I am convinced that God still uses 'the foolishness of our proclamation to save those who believe' (1 Corinthians 1:21). Preaching is still a powerful weapon in God's armoury, but we must find appropriate ways of doing it for the present age. Leslie Weatherhead used to say that the aim of preaching was 'making God real and changing the lives of men and women'[3]. That must still be our aim. I propose therefore to demonstrate the need for Biblical preaching and then to offer some clues as to how we can do this more effectively.

We need to re-discover the place of teaching in the life of the Church.
One of the greatest needs of the Church today is for taught Christians who know what we believe, and why we do so. Good teaching inspires confidence and so helps us, not only to live the life of discipleship ourselves, but also to share the faith with others.

Over recent years, we have seen a dramatic decline in the number of children attending Sunday school, and the consequent demise in its influence. For too long we have tacitly assumed that Religious Education in schools was a means of communicating the claims of Christ so that children would have enough knowledge to decide for themselves, whether or not they wish to take the Christian faith seriously. Very much aware of the needs of a multi-cultural society, RE teachers now seek to help children understand the significance of the religious quest, no matter what form it might take. The result is that often our children leave school with a little information about the variety of world religions, but no real understanding of any of them. Aware of the dangers of proselytism, educators are rightly keen to avoid it.

---

[3] Quoted by Turner, J. M. *The Expository Times* (January 2000) p. 114

Christians can hardly expect others, especially non-believers, to prepare children for Christian faith. This is the responsibility of the family and the church. Unfortunately, the family is often ill-equipped to do it, and, all too often, the Church ignores the need and so does nothing to meet it.

Adult education in the Church is in serious need of rejuvenation. Class Meetings have largely disappeared and, although some of our house groups are excellent, others leave a lot to be desired. Some even degenerate into groups for the 'pooling of ignorance' rather than the 'sharing of faith'. In many churches there are no opportunities for mid-week teaching and fellowship and often little hunger for the discovery of greater depths of discipleship.

It is not surprising therefore that there is a high level of biblical illiteracy and that few see the Bible as relevant. People tend to believe 'what feels right', irrespective of whether or not it is in harmony with the teaching of scripture[4]. Preachers today must start where the people are, deal with the questions they are asking and unpack the message of the Bible in such a way that their hearers cannot escape its relevance for today.

Although the need for Christian education is enormous, the Sunday sermon is in many churches the only opportunity we have for expounding the scriptures, teaching the great doctrines of the faith and helping people see their relevance for contemporary living. Our preaching, therefore, must retain its teaching content. We need to help our people grow in their faith and so enable them to face the deepest questions of life from a Christian perspective.

This presents us with a problem, for preaching is not primarily a teaching medium, nor is it the best way of

---

[4] Smith, Paul *Digging for Treasure* (Ilkeston: Moorleys, 2012) p. 6

communicating knowledge. Its aim is much broader. It seeks to stimulate the response of the whole person to the message of the gospel. Effective preaching, says Colin Morris, 'grips our imagination, then convinces our reason, arrests our conscience and finally reinforces our will, so that stage by stage we have made a fully human response to God's word'[5].

I believe that the growth of the church always begins with a deeper spiritual life. Good preaching that is divinely inspired, well delivered, life-related and thoroughly Biblical will bring new life to our churches and enable us to be more effective in mission, ministry and evangelism.

Leander Keck, an American New Testament scholar, reminds us that every renewal of Christianity has been accompanied by a renewal of preaching. Each renewal of preaching, in turn, has rediscovered Biblical preaching[6].

In his 2011 *Digging for Treasure* lecture, Richard Bewes shared a healthy anatomy of a sermon. Beginning with a text, a main theme, an aim and an introduction, it then needs:
- **Bones:** A framework that will do justice to the flow of the passage.
- **Flesh:** The filling out of the main substance.
- **Wings:** The personal and imaginative touches that will make the sermon live.
- **Teeth:** The bite, the challenge and the application.[7]

That's not a bad starting point for us as we explore preaching for the twenty-first century.

---

[5] Morris, Colin *Raising the Dead* (London: Fount, 1996) p. 27
[6] Quoted in Quicke, Michael *360 Degree Preaching* (Grand Rapids, Michigan: Baker Academic, 2003) p. 29
[7] Bewes, Richard *Digging for Treasure* (Ilkeston: Moorleys, 2011) p. 17

What do we mean by Expository Preaching?

Although I have always regarded myself as a Biblical preacher, I have never described my sermons as 'expository'. Many who claim that distinction believe in a 'verse by verse' method, which they think interprets scripture most accurately. However, unless it is done really well, it can sound as though the preacher has swallowed his favourite commentary for breakfast and now proceeds to regurgitate it for the congregation. I have never found such an approach helpful. Listening to such preaching can be tedious, and I have sometimes found it difficult to sort out the wood from the trees.

It was a great relief, therefore, when I discovered the approach of Haddon Robinson, an American Professor of Homiletics, who said that the 'verse by verse' approach was only one among many ways of doing expository preaching. He states that expository preaching 'at its core is more a philosophy than a method'. The important thing is that we endeavour to bend our thought to the scriptures rather than use the Bible to support our opinions. Exposition is primarily a matter of being 'exposed' to the message of scripture and 'exposing' hearers to its power[8].

With that renewed understanding, I can enthusiastically agree with John Stott who believed that all true Christian preaching should be expository. He reminds us that 'to expound scripture is to bring out of the text what is there and expose it to view. The expositor prizes open what appears to be closed, makes plain what is obscure, unravels what is knotted and unfolds what is tightly packed'[9].

---

[8] Quoted in Quicke, Michael *360 Degree Preaching* (Grand Rapids, Michigan: Baker Academic, 2003) p. 28

[9] Quoted in Wiltshire, John *Digging for Treasure* (Ilkeston: Moorleys, 2011) p. 21

In our 2012 *Digging for Treasure* Conference, Paul Smith shared his conviction that, 'Any preaching which is worthy of the name Christian, must involve some element of Biblical exposition. Our primary task as preachers is to take and apply the truths of scripture to the hearts, minds and lives of the hearers in such a way that they are stimulated by God's truth and challenged to act in accordance with God's will'[10]. In short, we are called to be Biblical preachers.

This helpful and holistic view of our task, reflects the views of many who write about preaching and teach others to communicate the gospel effectively. As W.E. Sangster put it, 'Exposition merely means setting forth or explaining' to 'lay the meaning bare'[11].

Haddon Robinson explores the implications of Expository preaching when he defines it as 'the communication of a Biblical concept, derived from and transmitted through a historical, grammatical and literary study of a passage in its context, which the Holy Spirit first applies to the personality and experience of the preacher then, through the preacher, applies to the hearers'[12].

Obviously this is an approach to preaching that is thoroughly Biblical and much needed today.

When I was Superintendent Minister of Methodist Central Hall, Westminster, we were asked by *The Times* to host their annual *Preacher of the Year* competition and I was asked to be Chairman of the Panel of Judges. Each year this necessitated my reading well over a hundred sermons and

---

[10] Smith, Paul *Digging for Treasure* (Ilkeston: Moorleys, 2012) p. 5

[11] Sangster, W.E. *The Craft of the Sermon* (London: Epworth, 1954) p. 59, 61

[12] Quoted in Quicke, Michael *360 Degree Preaching* (Grand Rapids, Michigan: Baker Academic, 2003) p. 26

listening to the finalists. Some of them were extremely good Biblical expositions, but had hardly any clear contemporary application. Others were clearly life related, helpful and relevant but, although they might quote an occasional Biblical verse, there was no in-depth exploration of the text and its background. I came away with the impression that good preaching should not be either good exposition or a Christian reflection on contemporary issues - it needs to be both. Based on a thorough and profound Biblical exegesis, the message can be clearly related to the real life issues we have to face today. Then we are not only dealing with modern concerns, but also demonstrating the relevance of scripture and showing how it helps us live as disciples today. Perhaps that is what Donald English meant when he stressed the preacher's need to have 'one foot in scripture and one foot in the world and to take the strain between the two'.

The Preacher's Authenticity.
Donald English often said that we didn't need more arguments for the Christian faith. Rather we needed more free samples! He was referring to 'Christians who so radiate the love of Christ that the message shines through them'. That is particularly true for preachers. Years ago, a minister reminded me that to be a preacher, one needs:
    a heart for the people of God
    a desire for the glory of God
    a hunger for the Word of God
    a dependence on the Spirit of God
    a love for the Son of God
    and a burden for those without the knowledge of God.

Especially in matters of religion, people have no time for pretence or hypocrisy. The preacher must therefore be authentic. Bishop Phillips Brooks defined preaching as the 'portrayal of truth through personality'. 'The truth must really come through the person, not merely over his lips.'

Preachers should relate to their congregations 'with such close contact, that the Christ who has entered into their lives may, through them, enter into that of their hearers'.

Martin Luther, the Protestant reformer, reminds us, 'We inform when we pass on bits of knowledge,' but 'We communicate when we disclose something of ourselves in the act of passing on bits of knowledge. We cannot divorce our words from our own personal discipleship.'

Similarly, William Quayle pointed out that, 'Preaching is the art of making a preacher and delivering that'. 'The sermon is the preacher up to date'.

Educators suggest that much of what we learn comes through the personality of the communicator, rather than the content of the teaching. If a communicator is popular, students tend to learn more, but if they do not like the teacher, they hear little of what is said. It is estimated that 55% of what we learn comes through the body language of the teacher, 38% through the tone of voice and only 7% through the words used. Within 24 hours, most people forget 60% of what they have learned and another 15% is lost within the next 24 hours. Our task therefore may be difficult, but it is not impossible. Even though we live in a highly visual age, there is still a place for the spoken word and the skills of oratory. We may, though, need to update and improve our communication skills.

Communication skills for a visual age.

It had been well said that every preacher should be like 'Moses with the message of God in his heart and mind and Aaron with the skills of speech'. Back in the fourth-century BC, Demosthenes, the great Athenian statesman and orator said, 'The three requisites for oratory are, delivery, delivery, delivery!'

Marketing experts and advertisers seek to attract, inform and persuade. They know the importance of good packaging and we can learn much from them. Good content can be ruined by poor delivery, whereas less inspiring content can really inspire if it is freshly delivered and made to sound interesting. So let's look at some of the tools that help us get the message across.

The power of Illustration.
Although his material was superb, the older minister's delivery was monotonous and boring, so he was difficult to listen to. He became ill, so asked his young colleague to stand in for him at the church's midweek fellowship and suggested that in view of the short notice, he might read the address already prepared. As the paper was being read, the audience sat up and obviously began to take notice. Afterwards they thanked him and said, 'It was so much better than we get from our own minister'. He replied, 'But I was reading what your minister wrote. It's just that I opened a few windows!'

That's what illustrations do: open windows to let the light in! Or, as W.E. Sangster put it: 'They serve as lampposts along the road of understanding, lighting up what might otherwise be only dimly understood'. They secure the congregation's attention, illuminate ideas and relate the gospel to the ordinary experiences of life.

Although people might well forget much of what we say, they will often remember a good illustration. This is because most of us are more likely to listen emotionally and visually, than intellectually.

Illustrations do, though, need to be used with care.

Remember that:
- 'Some of the best illustrations are in the Bible'.
- The 'way in' to an illustration is vital. We have to convince the congregation that we have something worth listening to.
- Illustrations must not be threatening or confrontational.
- A telling story with a strong punch-line can encapsulate a profound truth and make it live.
- Humour can rest the congregation and so prepare it to move on to a new aspect of the truth being shared.
- Each major point requires an illustration.

In considering an illustration, ask yourself the following:
- Does it engage the hearer and stimulate both imagination and intellect?
- Does it really illustrate the point or is it just a good story?
- Is it the servant or the master?
- Does it sound convincing?
- Is it reinforcing the fact that the gospel is about the whole of life?

Colin Morris points out that, 'the human mind is not so much a debating chamber where we argue about ideas, as a picture gallery around which we hang our images of the world'.[13]

The Use of Imagery.
The Bible is full of stories that are a great resource for preachers. A story can often carry a particular image that sticks in the memory. It can touch the depths of our being, our thoughts, feelings and will and so motivate a change of lifestyle. Such an image can become the focus of prolonged

---
[13] Morris, Colin *Raising the Dead* (London: Fount, 1996) p. 19

reflection, and so stimulate growth in understanding and a more thorough application to life.

Instead of looking for the main idea or key thought in a passage, it is sometimes good to search for the dominant image and explore that in such a way that it touches, thought, feeling and imagination. Such a sermon is not so much an explanation of the scriptures but a process of imaginatively entering into their world and then using that world as a lens to look out onto our world today.

Make the familiar strange.
A former Professor of mine drummed into us the need for preachers to 'make the familiar strange'. Often our listeners think they know the gospel. Therefore they expect little from the sermon. The more predictable the message, the less impact it has. We need to surprise them with a new insight or help them see old truths in a new light. Then what might well have become stale and hackneyed can come across with new life and urgency. Young people in particular need to feel alive, so we dare not make the faith sound oppressive, irrelevant or boring.

As Colin Morris reminds us: 'The basic purpose of Jesus' preaching was not to enlighten us but to shock us awake, to rock us out of the comfortable tramlines of our habitual existence and get us to face another way'[14].

Preaching is hard work, but it's worth the effort.
Writing in 1911, J. H. Jowett said, 'Preaching that costs nothing accomplishes nothing. If the study is a lounge, the pulpit will become an impertinence'.

---

[14] Morris, Colin *Raising the Dead* (London: Fount, 1996) p. 38

General guidelines for preachers:

1) Read widely.
Don't only read books written by those who agree with you. Remember that no one does our mind larger service than a vigorous and dangerous challenger, who forces us to look deeper into truths we have taken for granted.

A well-stocked mind gives new insight, leads to personal growth and gives more depth to our preaching. Fred Craddock, Professor of Preaching at the Candler School of Theology, Emory University, urged his students to start their preparation early. He used to remind them that in preparing to preach, their reading should be quite wide at the beginning of the week and then narrow down as they got nearer to Sunday. A Monday book, for example, might be a general introduction to the New Testament world. A Wednesday book could well be a commentary on the Gospel from which you will be preaching. But by Saturday, out of sheer desperation, you might turn to a book of other people's sermons from which you hope to steal some ideas and sermon illustrations. A week might not be the right length of preparation for all of us, but his point is well made.

2) Remember that the Bible was not written a verse at a time.
To look at a single verse only is akin to thinking that a single brush stroke is a painting. In reality, of course, that stroke is merely one of thousands skilfully arranged as the artist seeks an impressive total effect.

Back in the fourth-century, St. Athanasius said the Bible was 'like a mirror in which we learn the truth about ourselves, in the light of the God who made us, calls us and destines us for life'. Let the Scripture speak to you, before you start applying it to the needs of your congregation.

In sermon preparation always try to relate your text to its context. Explore its historical background. Why did the Bible writer put this particular verse or passage in its present place? What was its significance when it happened? What would it mean to those who first heard it read? What does it mean for us today?

When reading the gospels, for example, consider the words of Jesus when he spoke them. Why did the gospel writer link them with what has gone before, and what follows? How would they have been understood by the first generations of Christians against the background of their culture and the circumstances in which they found themselves? Such background knowledge will help us relate the message to the needs of today.

3) Gather resources for future use and file them carefully so they are easy to find.
One of the best things I ever did when I began my ministry was to start a card index in which I noted illustrations, quotes, and points that I might like to develop into a sermon later. They are each given a subject heading, such as 'prayer', 'faith', 'Bible', 'Easter', 'Remembrance', etc. It's also helpful to note the source of the material. By now the index is enormous, but I still use it regularly. Especially when pressed for time, I have been able to use the fruit of my reading, or reflect on experiences that I recorded months or even years ago.

I also have an index of Bible Reference cards. I might have read something about Isaiah that inspired me, but was not particularly relevant to the sermon I was preparing then on chapter 40. It might, though, be very helpful if I wanted to work on chapter 55, so I did not want to forget it. It was therefore recorded for future use. It's also good to have a 'sermon seed' box, in which insights that might come in later can be stored, until you are ready develop them into a sermon.

Nowadays, all of these things can be done at least as well, and probably better, on a computer but I certainly do recommend the basic idea.

4) I hear, I forget.   I see, I remember.   I do, I understand.
Educators remind us how good teaching enables us to learn. Try to establish a relationship with your hearers. Engage them. Encourage them to join you in a voyage of discovery as you explore a theme together. Although you may be the only speaker, your questions and the way you involve them in thinking things through, enables them to take part in the learning process and so enables them to remember what they have learned. We need conversation partners not a passive audience.

5) Preaching should always be positive.
Even though sometimes we need to challenge, we also need to build up. Our people need to feel valued and loved. A sermon should tell people 'how to get on', not 'where to get off'. As W.R. Maltby wrote, 'You preach the gospel, therefore: No demand without the gospel: No diagnosis without the cure: One word about sin, ten for the Saviour'.

6) Remember that no sermon is strong, which is not strong in structure too.
A good sermon needs:
- Movement or it won't hold attention.
- Progress as each point is developed to lead on to the next one.
- A landing field, which you have selected in advance. Otherwise you will circle around not knowing where and when to quit.

7) In Sermon delivery, never underestimate the value of 'a well timed pause'.
Mark Twain rightly said that, used wisely, it 'carries more weight than the spoken word'.

From Desk to Pulpit.
Now a few thoughts based on personal experience and insight and gained from so many sources both written and spoken that have helped me learn what it means to 'preach the Word'.

1) Choose the passage or the text.
Several days before you are due to preach, begin by reading the lectionary readings, the passages you have been given or the ones you have chosen. That will give you time to digest the Biblical material and also to reflect prayerfully on both the Biblical context and how it relates to contemporary needs. Prayerfully read it aloud. Then re-read it several times.

2) Meditate on it.
Try to sink deeply into the passage to be really clear what it is saying. Pray over it. Live with it. Wait, absorb, watch, wonder and catch the vision. Let your unconscious mind work on it. Remember that, having begun your preparations early, you will be on the look out for illustrations all the time.

3) Enjoy a period of free association.
What does the passage say to you? Analyse it. Explore its context. What is its relevance and application? What ideas or illustrations might be useful? Make brief notes. Then consult the commentaries and perhaps a Bible dictionary. Read widely, looking for grains of truth that will make the sermon live.

4) Isolate the dominant thought.
What is the overriding thrust of the passage? Reflect on its outstanding truth and its distinctive message. Draw out and develop the main point of the sermon and let it live for the congregation.

In construction any building needs scaffolding but, once finished, the public only need to see the building itself. A thorough analysis of the Biblical material is extremely helpful to the preacher who really wants to understand the text, but some of it is like the scaffolding needed to erect the building. The congregation does not want you to share everything you have learned. They only need to hear the finished product.

5) Interpret the dominant thought for the needs of today.
What did it mean then, and what does it say now? How do other insights in the passage clarify or illustrate the main point? Especially if you are using the lectionary, focus on one passage, and use your other Bible readings to illustrate its key message. Decide on the aim of your sermon, and write it down.

6) Design the sermon.
Write your aim at the top of your notes. What are you trying to do for/with these people? Then, begin with a rough outline. In expounding a passage it is helpful to arrange your points in the order in which they occur in the passage. If you unfold its truth in manageable bite-sized pieces it is more likely to be remembered and applied. All your material should serve the dominant thought. Be disciplined and ask yourself if a particular idea or illustration really helps the argument. Then have the courage to cut out material that's not absolutely necessary. Your message needs to be sharp, clear and to the point.

Always keep your aim in mind. Ask yourself:
- Is this life-related and relevant?
- Are there sufficient good illustrations?
- Will the order in which I have presented my points enable them to have maximum effect?
- Have I helped the congregation know why this message is important and how they can do something about it?

In our 2012 conference, Paul Smith shared some very helpful clues as to how our points can be developed to maximum effect. He suggests that if we reveal the greatest truths too early, the later parts of the sermon will be an anti-climax. We need to take our congregations with us on a journey of discovery. It is good, therefore, to reveal the secondary truths first, and then work towards a climax of the revelation, which lies at the heart of the passage. It is good to work from the general to the specific. Thus, we move from a broad embrace of the truth to the impact it should have on individuals.

He also suggests that each point should include exposition, application and illustration

7) Add the Introduction and Conclusion.
If these are effective, the whole sermon will benefit and the hearers will be more likely to remember and apply some of the truths you have sought to share. The introduction must say what the subject is and why it matters. It should catch the attention and make the congregation feel, 'This is going to be worth hearing!'

The conclusion should not contain any new material. It should be clear, brief, to the point and build up to a climax that emphasizes the aim. It is good to finish with an illustration that will hammer the point home. Alternatively we can ask, or pose, questions which will involve the congregation in deciding how they will respond to the message they have received.

8) Write down and pray over your sermon - and so prepare yourself.
Preach it aloud to yourself, so that as you hear it you can make subtle changes and improvements. It's good to prepare a full manuscript, but if you can preach from notes, do so. This keeps you on track, but gives you a more natural flow and allows more eye contact with your hearers.

9) Deliver the sermon.
Memorize the sermon structure. Highlight the main points so that they stand out when you quickly glance at them. Rely on the Holy Spirit during delivery. As an old black preacher puts it: **'I reads myself full, thinks myself clear, prays myself hot, then I lets go!'**

Conclusion
In a little country chapel, on the top of the pulpit desk, deliberately placed in full view of the preacher, there is a text that reminds us of our calling as preachers, and why our congregations come to church: **'Sir, we would see Jesus' (John 12:21).** It is an enormous privilege to preach the gospel and that must always be our aim. As we lead worship and share the Word, may they always see Christ.

PREACHING APOCALYPTICS
Steve Brady
Principal, Moorlands Bible College

A young undergraduate at the University of Cambridge had never read the Bible before he was given a New Testament. When he read it, he commented, 'It was a bit repetitious at the beginning, but I did enjoy the science-fiction at the end!' No, he was not being facetious. Rather, he was trying to slot the book of Revelation into some kind of literary category, a *genre*, he could understand. This is, in fact, a very sensible thing to do when we come to any part of the Bible, and something that many Christians fail to give attention to. Sadly, too many approach the Bible with a flat-footed literalness that attempts to explain all the books in the same way as if, for example, they were all epistles or parables. However, Scripture contains many different types of literature: poetry and prose; history and prophecy; promises and principles, parables and laments, etc. Failing to recognise a book's literary genre can land the reader in all sorts of trouble. Allow me to illustrate.

First, we turn to a rather well known example from Church History that illustrates the point, and that rather painfully. Origen of Alexandria (185-254 AD) was an outstanding philosopher/theologian. However, when he read our Lord's words about those who for the sake of the kingdom had 'made themselves eunuchs' (Matthew 19:12), he interpreted it literally, and was subsequently castrated – ouch! Or think of a more contemporary illustration concerning children. A well-known proverb proclaims: 'Train a child in the way he should go, and when he is old he will not turn from it' (Proverbs 22:6).

How many Christian parents have tormented themselves when their child has become the proverbial 'prodigal'. If they had trained the child properly, surely they would not have gone off the rails. The result? Often tortured, guilt-laden parents, who then hope that the meaning is that when their child is old, perhaps they will return to the fold. Perhaps. However, in order to understand the book of Proverbs, it is important to realise that although it does contain promises[15], it generally contains principles. Moreover, some of the principles that the book promotes seem to stand in direct contradiction with one another:

> Do not answer a fool according to his folly,
> or you will be like him yourself.
> Answer a fool according to his folly,
> or he will be wise in his own eyes.
> (Proverbs 26:4-5)

So, the Bible contradicts itself? No. But this is the book of *Proverbs*. We British folks have our own proverbs that seem equally contradictory: 'Many hands make light work'; 'Too many cooks spoil the broth'. Which is true? On one occasion, I was questioning my students about the seeming contradiction posed by Proverbs 26:4-5. I asked them how they would respond to the first one, 'Do not answer a fool'. One bright spark quipped, 'We're not answering you!' Of course, you should not try to get the last word with a Liverpudlian like me. So, I retorted, 'Hey, what a way to fail your term paper! He who laughs last is the marker.' We will run into serious problems if we try to make all the proverbs into promises.

When we turn to the Book of Revelation, universally known as 'The Apocalypse', we discover that it is made up of several literary types, not just one. Some of it takes the form of an epistle. In fact, there are seven particular epistles, the

---

[15] e.g. the well-known Proverbs 3:5-6.

'letters to seven churches' with very specific messages and applications. If you want to trace that out in real detail, track down the work of the biblical scholar, Colin Hemer. He wrote an excellent commentary, containing a great deal of research into how these letters relate to the historical background and culture of the seven churches[16].

However, Revelation is also prophecy. In the opening verses of the book we are told:

> The revelation of Jesus Christ, which God gave him to show his servants what must soon take place. He made it known by sending his angel to his servant John, who testifies to everything he saw – that is, the word of God and the testimony of Jesus Christ. Blessed is the one who reads the words of **this prophecy**, and blessed are those who hear it and take to heart what is written in it, because the time is near. (Revelation 1:1-3)

What John is to record is also 'the revelation of Jesus Christ' (v1). The word 'revelation' is *apokalupsis,* from which our words 'apocalypse/apocalyptic' are derived. From it, we use apocalyptic to cover a literary genre that is found both in the Book of Revelation and other parts of the Bible. So what is apocalyptic? A scholarly reply would say something like: 'a literary form which developed firstly under the influence of the highly symbolic, prophetic apocalyptic'. Into this category fall such passages as Isaiah 24-27, written in the eighth century BC, Ezekiel 38-48, from the sixth century BC, and Daniel, which liberal scholarship has assigned to the second century BC, because of its high accuracy. But since

---

[16] Colin J Hemer, *The Letters to the Seven Churches of Asia in their Local Setting* (Sheffield:JSOT, 1986).

Scripture claims to be prophetic, along with many others, I am happy for it to be located in the sixth century BC. However, although Daniel has many apocalyptic features, Revelation is the only fully apocalyptic book in the Bible. Alongside it, passages like Matthew 24, Mark 13 and Luke 21 are also clearly apocalyptic. Without some knowledge of this genre, we may well spiritualise the literal and literalise the spiritual, thus making nonsense of the book. Pardon? Let me illustrate.

I once belonged to a denomination that loved to spiritualise the literal. Take the parable of the Good Samaritan, for example. What is it is really about? Being a good neighbour? Finding eternal life, perhaps? No, it is really about the Second Coming of Jesus any time soon! How come? Here's how. The real meaning of the parable is that, like the victim of the story, humanity has gone down from Jerusalem to Jericho, from the city of God to the city on the plain of destruction. All of us have fallen amongst thieves; the devil has robbed us. Religion came along, but it could not help us. Then the Good Samaritan came, who is obviously Jesus. He pours his blood and his Spirit (oil and wine) into our wounds to make us clean and renew us, and then he brings us into his Church (the inn) where the Holy Spirit (the innkeeper) looks after us. Of course, the two coins represent payment for two working days, and since *'With the Lord a day is like a thousand years, and a thousand years are like a day'*,[17] this means that the Lord is going to return in two thousand years' time. There's just one omitted character to mention from the Story of the Good Samaritan, the donkey. What does that represent? And anyone who believes a word of the foregoing!

So, we need to be careful when interpreting Scripture generally, and particularly when handling apocalyptic

---

[17] 2 Peter 3:8.

material. Accordingly, a few basic principles are necessary, and to them we turn.

Some Basic Principles for Handling Apocalyptic

1. Apocalyptic generally claims to reveal truths that readers could not arrive at by themselves.
It professes to be, as it suggests, a revelation from God, often delivered by an angelic or some other intermediary, telling the readers something they would not already know. It is important to understand that apocalyptic is not exclusively a Christian genre. This kind of literature, which is now becoming increasingly available in English translation, flourished between the second century BC and the second century AD. Jewish apocalyptic literature includes such books as 1 Enoch, The Sybilline Oracles, and the Apocryphon of Ezekiel. Later, other 'Christian' apocalypses, for example, the Apocalypse of Peter, would arise. So, what we can say is this: 'apocalyptic', though not called this at the time, was a way of expressing truth that was not alien to various readers at the time. Because it is not familiar to us does not mean that it was unfamiliar to them.

2. The language of apocalyptic is often highly esoteric and symbolic.
For example, we discover:
- frequent use of certain significant numbers: 3; 4; 7; 10; 12
- references to wild animals, often meaning foreign armies
- references to horns, e.g. 'the horn' and 'the great horn', which invariably mean kings, kingly authority, power
- stars, which often but not always refer to angels.

Apocalyptic literature is laden with symbolism because it was a kind of code, addressed to people going through very hard times, whose future was uncertain, and who needed to know that God had not forgotten them, but was working out his purpose, in spite of all the pointers to the contrary.

3. It is often deterministic, bordering on dualism.
Apocalyptic literature is written in such a way that it seems as if nothing can change what is about to happen. There is an inevitability about it. It is a very black and white view. Of course, some Christians are like this about the will of God, which is so determinative that one can only sing, *Que sera, sera*, 'whatever will be will be'. But the Bible, in general, is not deterministic. It emphasises God's sovereignty and our human responsibility and accountability - simultaneously. However, there is in apocalyptic the suggestion that this is the way things will be, and nothing will change them.

Ways of interpreting the book of Revelation
There are no short cuts to understanding the book of Revelation, but there are some traditional routes into it, which it can be helpful for us to understand. The following statement by the great intertestamental scholar, R. H. Charles, can act as an encouragement for us to undertake the hard work such study requires: 'Once the symbolism of the book of Revelation is understood it is easier to interpret than the epistle of Romans'.

1. The Preterist route
Since 'preterist' means 'to do with the past', this line of interpretation recognises the value of understanding the historical and cultural background at the time the book was written. Now this is always a good, sound principle for understanding any part of the Bible. We ask, what did the book mean to its original hearers? What did they make of it? Presumably they did not regard it as gibberish and nonsense. If it had not communicated to them, why would they have treasured it and retained it within the canon of Scripture? We need, therefore, to understand ways in which it made sense

to them. So, by way of illustration, from a preterist perspective, let us turn to Revelation 3:16, addressed to the church at Laodicea: 'So, because you are lukewarm – neither hot nor cold – I am about to spit you out of my mouth'.

A standard interpretation, which I fear I may have preached in the past, is that Jesus wants His followers either to be totally for Him or totally against Him. The last thing He wants is for people to sit on the fence. People should nail their colours to the mast and, taken to its logical extreme, if they are against Him, they should go out and start killing Christians or something, a bit like Paul before his conversion. However, this interpretation has to be weighed against other scriptures such as, 'A bruised reed he will not break, and a smouldering wick he will not snuff out',[18] which seem to suggest that even a little faith in a great God is better than a lot of faith in a small one. Is Jesus saying that he wants nothing to do with those of weak faith? No, he is not. Here the preterist approach can help us as we begin to understand more about the city of Laodicea.

Laodicea was situated in the Lycus valley. Not far away, at Hierapolis, there were hot, refreshing springs and, at Colossae, there were cold, refreshing waters. Due to the fact that it was built on sandstone, Laodicea had the reputation of having the worst water in the empire. The water there was vile. It was lukewarm and tasted horrible. If you drank it, you wanted to spit it out immediately. The Laodicean Church thought that they had achieved mega-church status; they thought they had made it: 'You say, "I am rich; I have acquired wealth and do not need a thing"' (3:17). They were likewise very proud of their achievements as a church. But Jesus has a very different view: 'But you do not realize that you are wretched, pitiful, poor, blind and naked' (3:17).

---

[18] Isaiah 42:3.

His reference to being blind is again very pointed, for there was a famous eye centre in Laodicea. So, Jesus is not saying that he wishes that the Laodicean Christians were either for him or against him. Rather, as we might say today, he would that they were as cheering as a hot chocolate on a winter's night, or as refreshing as iced lemonade on a hot day. We can then immediately grasp that understanding the background of the text can be most helpful in arriving at an accurate interpretation.

2. The Historicist route
This has also been called the Protestant view, because it stems from the sixteenth century Reformation understanding that the beast in Revelation 13, whose number is 666, was none other but the Pope of Rome, and the city set on seven hills was Rome[19]. It is a view still held by some Protestants today. Inherent in this view is the idea that the unfolding drama of God's redemption is actually taking place in Western Europe, i.e. we are the centre of the action!

I once heard the famous New Testament scholar, D. A. Carson, remark that the great New Testament scholar, F. F. Bruce, believed that John Calvin had omitted to write on the Book of Revelation for a very good reason. John Calvin was an outstanding theologian for two reasons: he was a brilliant exegete of the Bible, able to subject the text to the microscope, as it were. In addition, he also was a brilliant 'big picture' man – what we call a 'systematician', a systematic theologian. He could see both the big picture and the detailed one: it is often unusual for one individual to have both these skills. Why then did Calvin not write on the book of Revelation? F. F. Bruce expressed the view that Calvin was too good a theologian to try to make the text of Revelation apply to the Roman Catholic Church in sixteenth-century Europe! Therefore, not wanting to let his own side

---

[19] See Revelation 17:9.

down, he did not even try. I don't know whether this is true of Calvin, but it is a salutary warning when we think 'this equals that'.

3. The Symbolical/Idealist route

This approach acknowledges that the book of Revelation is full of symbols, intended to be illustrations of the truth, and not necessarily the truth themselves. We can draw an analogy with the characters Gandalf and Frodo in Tolkien's immensely popular *Lord of the Rings*. Although they themselves are not real, they illustrate important aspects of truth, loyalty, bravery, availability, etc.

Likewise, imagine for a moment that someone who has never been to the cinema before, let alone to a science fiction film, is taken to see *Star Wars*, and asked to write down everything that happens, whilst the film runs on. When the viewer comes out from the film, he has to find ways of expressing all the unusual characters he has seen such as Chewbacca and Darth Vadar, all in imaginary worlds, as well as all the details of the plot. Then imagine what somebody reading his account two hundred years later, who is also not familiar with science fiction, might make of it. This, it is urged, is precisely what is happening in the book of Revelation. John is seeing a revelation played out before him via a vision and is told to write down what he is seeing[20]. He is faced with the very real challenge of having to convey in word pictures images and symbols that he has seen. A daunting task!

4. The Dispensationalist route

Dispensationalists believe that the Church will be whisked away to be with Jesus before the Tribulation (see 1 Thessalonians 4:17, and Revelation 4:1). Therefore, from chapter 6 through to chapter 19, Revelation does not apply to

---

[20] Revelation 1:19

Christians, as they have been raptured to be with Christ. While what is happening in these chapters is interesting from a theoretical point of view, it will not affect us as Christians directly, but has more to do with the Jewish remnant, converted to Christ during this period. It is the view expounded by the Scofield Reference Bible, and the hugely popular *Left Behind* series of Tim LaHaye. It is a widely held position, especially in North America and, since it has huge implications for Israel and the Middle East, has had a huge influence on American policy in that region of the world.

5. The Moderate Futurist route
This approach believes the future is still unfolding; all the events of Revelation, the Second Coming excepted, have not happened in the past, as per a Preterist reading of the text might suggest. So, as we approach the end of time we should see more and more of the events prophesied in Revelation coming to pass on the earth, including the rise of the Anti-Christ, the Great Apostasy, and a period of intense tribulation, the Great Tribulation.

Summary
Here, then, are five major ways in which the book of Revelation is interpreted. Let me sum up this section by looking briefly at how four prominent biblical scholars approach the book.

Warren Wiersbe, in his *Be Victorious* commentary, uses a Dispensational framework, suggesting a very simple outline. In his view, the book has three sections: what has been (chapters 1-3), what is (4-5), and what shall be (5-22).

From a previous generation, William Hendricksen, sought to demonstrate that Revelation is based on the contrapuntal principle, and that there are actually seven parallel sections. In music contrapuntalism is a device whereby successive layers of music are built into a harmonious whole. In

Hendricksen's view, Revelation describes seven scenes of the same event, but each from a slightly different angle, so presenting a successively layered complete picture. Thus, the book should not be seen as sequential (a chronological account starting at the beginning), but as thematic (it keeps coming back to the same event again and again). In the same groove as Hendricksen sits Michael Wilcock's *I saw Heaven Opened*.[21] He deviates from Hendriksen in suggesting that Revelation actually has eight scenes. Since a Jewish boy was circumcised when he was eight days old, and Jesus rose from the dead on the eighth day (having died on the sixth day and been buried on the seventh day), he sees eight as the number signifying a new beginning. In his interpretation, the eighth scene is chapters 21 and 22, which is ultimately about the new beginning of a New Heaven and a New Earth.

George Beasley-Murray emphasises the overall picture of Revelation in his fine commentary. He says, 'It was not written to hold threats of damnation before sinners but to encourage saints to press on despite all opposition, and to win the inheritance. The Revelation was written that men might enter the city of God, and the vision of the city is the true climax of the book.'[22]

Moving Forward
As we seek to decide for ourselves what is the best way to approach the book of Revelation, I think it is vital to remember what I said earlier about literary genres. Different literary genres are appropriate to different types of subject matter. When it comes to handling an account of an individual's life, for example, the narrative style is most appropriate. As we read the story of David's life, we are able

---

[21] Wilcock, M. *The Message of Revelation: I saw Heaven Opened* (London: IVP, 1975)
[22] Beasley-Murray, G. *The Book of Revelation* (London: MMS, 1974)

to come to an understanding of him as a complex character, who was both 'a man after God's heart' and also capable of adultery and murder. This can be strangely encouraging for many of us who see similar ambiguities in our own lives. However, earlier explained, the apocalyptic genre works in black and white, although in Revelation there is a great deal of Technicolor in the detail! It does not deal too well with ambiguities. The subject matter with which it is dealing is extremely serious and requires that people should make up their mind one way or the other – either for Jesus or for Satan. Running through the Book is the underlying question: whom do you worship, whom do you serve?

Another important aspect of apocalyptic is its ability to convey the transcendent, the otherness of God and the spiritual world. So, in the great central chapters 4 and 5, for example, we are given a glimpse into the throne room of God:

> And the one who sat there had the appearance of jasper and carnelian. A rainbow, resembling an emerald, encircled the throne. Surrounding the throne were twenty-four other thrones, and seated on them were twenty-four elders. They were dressed in white and had crowns of gold on their heads. From the throne came flashes of lightning, rumblings and peals of thunder.
> (Revelation 4:3-5)

It is an incredible and awesome scene. A few verses later, John describes how the four living creatures are constantly calling out, 'Holy, holy, holy!', echoing Isaiah 6, and reminding us that it is still the same God being worshipped. Then, John weeps and weeps as he observes the angel holding the scroll, which signifies the redemptive purposes of God, but who can find no one who is worthy to open it. The elders comfort him with the words, 'Do not weep! See, the

Lion of the tribe of Judah, the Root of David, has triumphed', but as he looks up expecting to see a lion, he sees 'a Lamb, looking as if it had been slain'[23]. I like to ask those who like to take the Bible literally whether they are expecting to see a literal lamb when they get to heaven, who is also a lion? Of course not! This is not a picture that is meant to be drawn, but a picture whose colourful imagery is meant to fire the imagination. The Old Testament is our grammar and phrasebook for the New Testament. Accordingly, the Lion is the '*Lion of the tribe of Judah*', who turns aside for no one, the true Davidic King, the long promised Deliverer. The Lamb is, of course, a picture of violent sacrifice, one who is the Redeemer, fulfilling all those types and shadows seen in the cultus of Israel's sacrificial system.

Now let's try to turn some of our principles into practice, if we may.

A case study: Revelation 12
At first sight, due to our unfamiliarity with apocalyptic, this is a most obscure passage:

> A great and wondrous sign appeared in heaven: a woman clothed with the sun, with the moon under her feet and a crown of twelve stars on her head. She was pregnant and cried out in pain as she was about to give birth. Then another sign appeared in heaven: an enormous red dragon with seven heads and ten horns and seven crowns on his heads. His tail swept a third of the stars out of the sky and flung them to the earth. The dragon stood in front of the woman who was about to give birth, so that he might devour her child the moment it was born.

---

[23] Revelation 5:5, 6

> She gave birth to a son, a male child, who will rule all the nations with an iron sceptre. And her child was snatched up to God and to his throne. (Revelation 12:1-5)

The first decision we have to make is whether this is a flashback to a previous time or a preview of what is taking place and will take place. Next, we need to decide who the cast of players in the scene are:

- *the woman giving birth*: at first sight it may seem obvious that the woman is the Virgin Mary but, since later in the chapter there is a reference to 'her offspring/seed'[24], it seems that she is intended to be a picture of the people of God through whom the Messiah would come, 'the desolate woman' who now bears children[25].
- *the dragon*: this is made easy for us because we are given the code in verse 9:
  > The great dragon was hurled down – that ancient serpent called the devil, or Satan, who leads the whole world astray. He was hurled to the earth, and his angels with him.

  Sometimes, in apocalyptic literature, we only need to read on a bit to discover what a particular symbol means.
- *the child*: the horrific picture of the dragon waiting to devour the child as soon as he is born is an allusion to attempts by Satan to destroy the promised Child. We immediately think, as Gospel readers familiar with the Christmas story, of Herod's murder of all infant boys under the age of two in Bethlehem. The child clearly refers to Jesus. His being snatched straight up to heaven, without any mention of his saving life, death or resurrection, is a bit of a surprise to us. But it should not be, given a moment's thought: the passage is emphasising

---

[24] Verse 17, 'seed' *(KJV)*
[25] See Isaiah 54:1

the utter oneness and completeness of the ministry of this Child. He is victorious.

The drama unfolds (verses 7-12), and we are told about the immediate consequences in the heavenly realms, flowing from Christ's completed work and ascension to God's throne: there is war in the heavenlies, the invisible, spiritual realm. The result is the casting down and out of Satan and his angels as they are hurled to the earth:

> Then I heard a loud voice in heaven say: 'Now have come the salvation and the power and the kingdom of our God, and the authority of his Christ. For the accuser of our brothers, who accuses them before our God day and night, has been hurled down'. (v. 10)

Through the birth of this Child, and his ascension to the throne, things have changed dramatically in the heavenly realm, and have momentous consequences for the earth:

> But woe to the earth and the sea, because the devil has gone down to you! He is filled with fury, because he knows that his time is short. (v. 12)

The spiritual warfare in the heavenlies sets off a spiritual chain reaction on earth. Why are things on earth at times so bad, so evil, so intensely wrong? Why does God get the blame for all the evil, even by those who profess not to believe in Him? The answer is the devil coming down to earth in great wrath because he knows his time is short.

Seventy years ago, on 6 June 1944, the Allied Forces began their liberation of Europe with the D-day landing, sustaining huge casualties in the battle for Normandy. Within just a few days, over a million men and thousands of tons of equipment had poured into Europe. It was the decisive battle of the Second World War. Meanwhile, of course, the Russians were also making progress, whilst the Americans were making their way up the boot of Italy. Although D-Day marked the beginning of the end, it was not yet the end. It would be almost a year before victory would be declared. With his days clearly numbered, did Adolf Hitler simply lay down his arms and surrender? No! Quite the contrary, all hell broke loose! Thousands more would have to die before his tyranny was finally defeated, though he knew his time too was short. The theologian, Oscar Cullmann, has used this period between the beginnings of victory and the final victory of the Second World War as a way of explaining the phase in cosmic history in which we as Christians are living out our lives. Cullmann explained that on the cross Jesus won the decisive battle, and we are now headed towards V-Day. But we have not arrived yet. The Christian is someone who lives between the times, the age that is passing and the age to come. We are still involved in raging and intense battles. The devil seems to win many of them: God in Jesus Christ wins the War! So, Christians have every reason to rejoice even in the midst of what, on earth, sometimes seems like overwhelming odds stacked against us: 'Those who are with us are more than those who are with them' (2 Kings 6:16). There are many things that we do not know, and are not meant to know. But here in Revelation 12 the curtain is drawn back far enough for us to know that there is spiritual warfare going on in the heavens. That part of the battle is not ours to fight: we are engaged in the battle that is being waged on earth – so keep praying on, keeping your armour bright (see Ephesians 6:10-20).

Some advice on preaching from the book of Revelation
In conclusion, I would like to give some advice to any preachers who are thinking about tackling Revelation.

Firstly, I would strongly advise that a preacher does not start a new pastorate by preaching on the book of Revelation. There is a temptation to want to start with a bang, but although the first few chapters may go quite well, by about chapter 6 you will probably wish you had never started. The book of Revelation can humble even the most experienced of preachers, so my advice to any preacher at the beginning of their preaching career would be to start on some of the more straightforward books of the Bible, or the (seemingly!) more clear parts of Revelation.

Secondly, before preaching from Revelation, get some acquaintance with this apocalyptic genre. Familiarise yourself with the books of Daniel, Ezekiel and Isaiah, the writers of which use similar timeframes and symbolism. Try to develop your own ideas about the patterns and symbolism of the book, which requires a certain amount of background reading and research. I have preached and lectured on this book more times than I can remember. Every time I do, I still come across something new and I wonder how I could have missed that before. So, before tackling the whole book of Revelation, it is perfectly acceptable to start with small sections of it, perhaps with the letters to the churches or some of the themes that run through it.

Thirdly, the preacher needs to make sure that they spend some time trying to work out the big picture of the book, before getting into the details because, as the saying goes, the devil is in the detail. To some people having to put in hours of study will be very boring, but it is impossible to get to grips with the book without it. So, humble yourself, and consult some of the excellent commentaries that are available, a few of which I list below.

Finally, it is possible to read Revelation and see only bowls, beasts, scarlet women and all the other vivid images and symbols that John describes. It is possible to read it and miss the biggest point of all: to see Jesus. He is the big story of Revelation. In chapter 1, we are given a revelation of the risen Lord. In chapters 2 and 3, we see him walking among the churches. In chapters 4 and 5, he is in the very centre of the throne room of God. And when we reach the end of the book we read:

> I did not see a temple in the city, because the Lord God Almighty and the Lamb are its temple. The city does not need the sun or the moon to shine on it, for the glory of God gives it light, and the Lamb is its lamp. (Revelation 21:22-23)

There is one word this 'Jesus-book' is insistent that we understand, 'Almighty'. The original, *pantocrator,* means 'ruler over everything'. It is used ten times in the Greek New Testament, and nine of those ten occur in Revelation (the other occurrence being 2 Corinthians 6:18), when it looked so dark and dim for the Church of Jesus. It is a reminder that no matter what is happening, God in Jesus is Lord on planet earth. The devil may seem to win so many battles, but God will win the war. God in Christ will overcome. We too, trusting in the blood of Jesus, testifying to his gospel, and laying down our lives if necessary to gain life indeed (Revelation 12:11), shall also overcome through Him who has loved us (Revelation 1:5).

For further reading:
Beasley-Murray G - *The Book of Revelation*
Bewes R - *The Lamb Wins!*
Hendriksen W - *More Than Conquerors*
Keener C – *Revelation*
Mounce R - *The Book of Revelation*
Osborne G - *Revelation*
Richardson J - *Revelation Unwrapped*
Wiersbe W - *Be Victorious*
Wilcock M - *I saw Heaven Opened*
Wilmshurst S – *The Final Word*

THE REFRESHING WORK OF THE HOLY SPIRIT[26]
Chris Blake
Principal, Cliff College

'All of them were filled with the Holy Spirit and began to speak in other languages, as the Spirit gave them ability.'
Acts 2:4 (NRSV)

Cliff College has had, from its earliest days, a focus on mission and evangelism and its motto, 'Christ for all – all for Christ', remains at the very centre of all that the College is and does. In 2012, the College was designated by the Methodist Conference as one of the two centres within the Methodist Discipleship and Ministries Learning Network and the College looks forward to offering our experience and expertise in the important areas of mission and evangelism to the wider Methodist Church through the work of the newly formed Network, as well as continuing with our many and varied links with students from a wide spectrum of denominational and non-denominational backgrounds.

Cliff College has been on its current site in Calver near Bakewell for 110 years, but its roots go back to the early 1880s and to the work of the Joyful News Mission. Thomas Champness, a Methodist Minister with a real heart for evangelism, had, more than twenty years previously, been on two occasions as a missionary to West Africa. His initial posting in 1857 was to Sierra Leone. Although he had candidated as a Methodist Minister, he was sent to Africa before he could start his training, and with only one year's experience as a fully accredited Local Preacher. He returned

---

[26] This is an extended version of a sermon delivered at the MET Celebration held during the Methodist Conference 2014

home in 1860 on furlough, having suffered with Yellow Fever. In 1862, having recovered his strength, Champness was sent back to West Africa, this time to Abeokuta in Nigeria. Sadly his wife, Mary Archer Champness, died from a fever after only a few months in the country. When I visited Nigeria in 2010, with a team from the Cliff College International Training Centre, I was able to visit her grave in Abeokuta and to remember the historical missionary vision given by God which was later to give rise to the work of Cliff College.

Thomas Champness became unwell again and so he returned once more to England where he served in several circuits before being appointed as a 'District Missionary', first in Newcastle-upon-Tyne and then in Bolton. In 1883, Thomas' commitment to evangelism led to the formation of the Joyful News Mission and to the production and sale of the *Joyful News* broadsheet newspaper. This was first published in February of that year, and was sold initially at a price of one halfpenny, with the profits initially going to the 'Worn Out Ministers Fund' and then later to support the training of young evangelists.

To celebrate the centenary of *Joyful News* in 1983, facsimile copies of the first edition of were produced. The first edition makes very interesting reading. On the front page there is an editorial item headed *Hints for those who write for this paper*. These hints include:

- Be interesting
- Never use two words when one will do
- Do not exaggerate
- Write on one side of the paper only
- If you are not an educated person do not worry about grammar or spelling; we will make it alright.

After this there are two lists:

What we want
- News of recent revivals
- Stories of remarkable conversions
- Answers to prayer
- Illustrations of providence

What we do not want
- Politics
- Controversy
- Connexional Finance

I make no comment about how the various elements included in those two lists are seen in the debates at the Methodist Conference! But I do note that this first edition of *Joyful News* is indeed full of details about recent revivals, stories of remarkable conversions, answers to prayer and illustrations of providence.

It is worth spending a few minutes just noting some of the many items of news from various places which were included in this first edition of 1883:

> Durham: Durham is being mightily moved just now. Our fifteen days' mission, which ought to have terminated yesterday, is to be continued another week. Many souls have been saved, and are giving strong evidence in public of the great change. Durham is proverbially a hard city, Methodism being comparatively weak in it; but there is at present an entire absence of prejudice. Our meetings are crowded with every class of people from the wealthiest to the poorest.

Chippenham: Opened my mission here on Sunday. Had a good beginning. Nearly a score of young people sought Jesus in the afternoon service. Open-air service at night and a chapel full of people and of power. An old man sought Jesus and several other adults. Many wounded. The town is divided this week between a wizard's entertainment, two corps of the Salvation Army, and our own mission. Oh for scores of souls.

Nenthead (Cumbria): Sunday was a glorious day in the Alston Circuit. After morning school I conducted a service, when 17 decided for Jesus. In the afternoon we had a time of refreshing from the presence of the Lord. At night, chapel crammed, the Lord of Hosts was with us. In the first service, 7 persons left their seats and came to the penitent rail seeking pardon, which all of them professed to find. We are still looking for greater things.

Arkwright Street Nottingham: Clouds of mercy gathered over this place on Sunday, and came down upon us in showers of blessing. The hand of the Lord was with us, of a truth. 80 upgrown persons and many children sought for mercy. Our congregation in the evening was magnificent – the chapel literally crammed, aisles and all. A day long to be remembered in Nottingham. 'O Jesus ride on'.

Corrbridge-on-Tyne: Glorious day on Sunday. I preached three times. The chapel was packed to its uttermost capacity. Had mighty and powerful times. Five souls saved, and many under deep conviction who did not come out.

> Sittingbourne: Commenced my mission here on Sunday. 10.30 excellent service. The Holy Spirit present in his sanctifying power. Many felt his influence resting on and filling them.

These reports, and there are many, many more of them, even in this first edition of 'Joyful News', are so exciting to read. Phrases such as 'Clouds of mercy gathered over this place', 'Had mighty and powerful times', 'A chapel full of people and power', and 'In the afternoon we had a time of refreshing from the presence of the Lord', speak of a real vibrancy and vitality of worship and describe an experience of profound and deep encounter with the holy and living God.

These accounts are exciting and wonderful, but they are perhaps different from what we see in many of our churches today. Of course, they describe events which took place over 130 years ago, and there are vast cultural and contextual differences between the world of 1883 and the world of 2014. However, the question still remains – are we today as open to the refreshing work of the Holy Spirit as we ought to be – and what exactly might it mean if we sought to live in that way?

Well there is clearly much that could be said about this vitally important subject – but I want to focus this evening on v. 4 from Acts 2 and simply highlight three ways in which that verse challenges and encourages us today. Let's remind ourselves of what that verse says: 'All of them were filled with the Holy Spirit and began to speak in other languages, as the Spirit gave them ability' (Acts 2:4).

So – three reflections on the refreshing work of the Holy Spirit as we look in turn at three of the phrases from within the verse that I have taken as our text.

1) The Holy Spirit: Refreshing Power for All

'All of them were filled with the Holy Spirit'

Acts 2 begins with a description of the believers gathered together on the day of Pentecost, and in the first 4 verses we are reminded repeatedly that that the experience of the filling with the Holy Spirit was for them all and not just for a select few.

So in Acts 2:1 we read, 'When the day of Pentecost had come they were *all* together in one place'. In v. 2 we read, 'And suddenly from heaven there came a sound like the rush of a violent wind, and it filled the *entire* house where they were sitting'. Similarly in v. 3, 'Divided tongues, as of fire, appeared among them, and a tongue rested on *each* of them'. And then we come to our text in verse 4 *'All* of them were filled with the Holy Spirit'.

The power of the Holy Spirit, which was poured out on the day of Pentecost on those who would form the beginnings of the church, was poured out on them *all*. They were *all* involved. Of course there are many different gifts, and different people are empowered in different ways, but the refreshing power of the Holy Spirit is for all.

Peter is recorded in Acts 2 as the one who stands up to preach, but Acts 2 is very clear that the others are standing with him (v. 14, 'But Peter *standing with the eleven*, raised his voice…'). Equally, at the end of the sermon (v. 37, 'Now when they heard this, they were cut to the heart and said to Peter *and the other apostles…*') it is equally clear that the crowd get into a conversation not just with Peter but also with 'the other apostles' as those in the crowd ask questions about what they need to do to respond to the preaching of the Good News of Jesus. The refreshing power of the Holy Spirit is for *all*. The question for us to ask is not *'Does God* want me to live in the refreshing power of the Holy Spirit?" but *'What will it mean* for me to live in that way?'

A few years ago, I was listening to a sermon preached in St Michael Le Belfrey in York. My wife Joy and I had been away for the weekend, and, on the way back to Cliff College, we stopped in York in order to attend the evening service there. It was a special mission weekend and the preacher was the Revd Dr Paul Weston who is on the staff at Ridley Hall in Cambridge and who has served as an external examiner for a PhD student at Cliff College.

It was Pentecost Sunday, and Paul Weston was preaching on a passage from John 16. The chapter is, of course, part of that powerful section of John's gospel which is full of amazing insights into the Trinity, as Jesus speaks with the disciples, and then prays to the Father about the sending of the Holy Spirit. Paul Weston drew our attention to v. 7, which I must admit I had not really faced before. In that verse, as his arrest and crucifixion are drawing nearer, Jesus says to his closest followers, 'Nevertheless, I tell you the truth: it is to your advantage that I go away, for if I do not go away the Advocate will not come to you; but if I go, I will send him to you'.

Paul Weston focussed on the phrase 'it is to your advantage' and invited us to reflect on how difficult it must have been for the first followers of Jesus to accept that: how could it possibly be to their advantage that Jesus would now leave them?

To illustrate this point, Paul told a story of something that had happened to him some time before. He was driving in his car following a motorcyclist. In front of them, the traffic lights turned to red. The motorcyclist stopped. Paul stopped in his car behind the motorcyclist and then, almost as if in slow motion, the motorcyclist tipped over and crashed to the ground. Paul quickly got out of his car and ran to see what, if anything, he could do. The motorcyclist picked himself up and assured Paul that all was well, and then, with a sheepish grin, said 'The thing is, for the last 16 years and until 2 days ago, I had a motorbike with a sidecar'.

For the first followers of Jesus it must have seemed that when Jesus spoke about 'going away' it would mean that all their support would be taken from them and they would go crashing to the ground. This surely must have been their first and foremost thought. And yet, as recorded in John 16:7, Jesus makes the astounding claim that it is actually *to their advantage* that he should go away. The reason for this statement is then clearly stated by Jesus as being the fact that he will send the power of the Advocate, the Holy Spirit, to come upon them all at that point in the future when he will no longer be physically at their side to support them. Amazingly, Jesus claims that this will be to their advantage.

The first followers of Jesus must have found this hard to accept, and perhaps we find it difficult to accept as well. Perhaps we sometimes imagine that it would have been so special to have lived in the 'Land of the Holy One' two thousand years ago, to have sat physically at the feet of Jesus, and to have listened to his teaching and to have witnessed at first hand his healing and cleansing power. Of course, this would indeed have been a wonderful experience, but when our imagination leads us to wish that we had lived two thousand years ago, we need to remember John 16:7 and hear again Jesus's words which claim that it is to our *advantage* that we live in the age when Jesus has sent the Holy Spirit in a powerful and refreshing way upon his followers.

I like the illustration used by Nicky Gumbel in the *Alpha* material, of the pilot light on a gas boiler in a central heating system. To be a gas boiler is to have a pilot light burning all the time, and to be a Christian is to have the gift of the Holy Spirit living in us all of the time, but that pilot light does not enable the gas boiler to fulfil its real function. Of course, you can look through the small viewing window and see the pilot light and often, if you put your hand on the outer casing of the boiler, you can sense some degree of warmth. However, it is only when the gas valve is opened up fully and the boiler bursts into full flame that the gas boiler really begins to fulfil its purpose. For the committed Christian, the question is not 'Have I received the Spirit?', but 'Have I allowed the Holy Spirit to fill my life with refreshing power?'

Peter, in his sermon which follows the outpouring of the Holy Spirit on the day of Pentecost, quotes from the prophet Joel, the image of the Spirit being poured out on 'all flesh' (Acts 2:17), poured out on sons and daughters, on young and old and on slaves, both male and female. The Holy Spirit is poured out *on all* with refreshing power and that includes each one of us. Jesus states that it is to our advantage that we live in this post-Pentecost age.

So firstly, the Holy Spirit: Refreshing Power for All.

2) The Holy Spirit: Refreshing Power for Transformation

'...as the Spirit gave them ability'

John Wesley in his *Thoughts upon Methodism,* published in 1786 wrote:

> I am not afraid that the people called Methodists should ever cease to exist either in Europe or America. But I am afraid, lest they should only exist as a dead sect, having the form of religion without the power. And this undoubtedly will be the case, unless they hold

fast the doctrine, spirit, and discipline with which they first set out.

These are familiar and vital words, but they are perhaps mild when compared to the writings of the Revd Samuel Chadwick who was a key person in the development of Cliff College. The first Principal of the College, Thomas Cook, died after 8 years in the post, and Chadwick was asked to become Principal, a role he fulfilled for twenty years.

In an article entitled *The Church without the Spirit*, published first in *Joyful News* and then included in a collection of such articles in a book called *The Way to Pentecost*, published in 1932 just after his death, we can read these words of Chadwick:

> The Spirit has never abdicated his authority nor relegated his power. Neither Pope nor Parliament, neither Conference nor Council is supreme in the Church of Christ. The Church that is man-managed instead of God-governed is doomed to failure. A ministry that is College-trained but not Spirit-filled works no miracles. The Church that multiplies committees but neglects prayer may be fussy, noisy, enterprising, but it labours in vain and spends its strength for nought. It is possible to excel in mechanics and fail in dynamic. There is a superabundance of machinery, what is wanting is power. To run an organisation needs no God. Man can supply the energy, enterprise and enthusiasm for things human. The real work of a church depends on the power of the Spirit.

Chadwick uses strong words and images in that paragraph. They are words which challenge us throughout the year, but they are words which perhaps challenge us particularly when we gather for our annual Methodist Conference. Perhaps I don't need to add much to Chadwick's words and so I simply to remind us of that final phase in our text in Acts 2:4, 'as the Spirit gave them ability'.

That phrase is a reminder that the refreshing work of the Holy Spirit is for transformation: for the transformation of our church both locally and Connexionally, and for the transformation of ourselves, the people of God who are to be transformed both individually and corporately.

The transformation which began on the day of Pentecost spread out geographically and rolled out through time. As we turn the pages of the Acts of the Apostles we see this over and over again as lives are changed, as communities are renewed and as the church is formed and re-formed in the refreshing power of the Holy Spirit.

For us individually, this is an on-going process. As I sit in my study at Cliff College, I can look out of the window over the terrace. At the side of the terrace is a bench dedicated to the memory of Donald and Bertha English. Every time I look at that bench I remember with thankfulness their shared ministry, and I remember Donald and his powerful preaching and I remember particularly the image he so often returned to, the image of the daily process of dying to self that we might rise to Christ. Although there may be particular moments when God works in our lives so that, in an instant, we take a significant step on the journey of discipleship, for most of us, for most of the time, that journey of discipleship will involve a daily process of placing ourselves in God's hands so that we might in each new day, die a little more to ourselves that we might rise a little more with Christ.

When I was in the sixth form at school, as a change from the "book work" of traditional A levels, we were encouraged, on a Wednesday afternoon, to participate in some form of sport or other activity. For half of each of the three terms, 'major sports' was compulsory: the first term football, the second term rugby and the third term cricket. The other half of each term could be used for a range of 'minor sports' such as horse riding and archery, or alternatively a more practical creative subject. During my two years of A level study, I tried my hand at both horse riding and archery, both with, I have to say, limited success! However, what sticks in my memory is the half-term I spent in the woodwork class. My maternal grandfather had been a carpenter and cabinet maker and in my younger childhood I spent many happy Sunday mornings in the shed behind the house where he lived making birthday and Christmas presents for other members of the family. This was an allowed activity on a Sunday morning as long as I was home for Sunday School which was then, of course, held in the afternoon. Only later did I realise that, although I thought that these presents were 'all my own work,' it was granddad who had brought the woodworking skills to the task and it was granddad who had performed all the difficult parts of the process. In my sixth form years I wanted to make something from wood that I could give to my Grandfather and Grandmother as a small token of thankfulness for those childhood experiences. And so I chose the woodwork class. The teacher quickly assessed my limited practical abilities and gave me a half-finished project to complete. This consisted of a rectangular block composed of different coloured pieces of wood stuck together. My task was, week by week, to place the rectangular block of wood on the lathe and, slowly but surely, shape it into a table lamp which, because of its shape, would enable the various colours of the wood to be seen.

It was not an easy process. I kept on making mistakes and the emerging table lamp would become misshapen as a chunk of wood flew off unexpectedly and unplanned. What was needed then was to place the block of wood back on the lathe and start again. The missing piece could not be replaced, but a new shape could be formed. It was a parable of the way in which when we make mistakes in our lives, we cannot always turn the clock back and go on as if nothing had happened. What we can do, however, is to place ourselves back on the lathe of God's love and allow his grace and power to work on us once more. What was very clear to me was that the shaping of the block of wood only took place when it was on the lathe. In the store cupboard from one Wednesday to the next, nothing happened. If we want to allow God to shape our lives, we cannot remain in the store cupboard of trying to change ourselves in our own strength. To be transformed involves dying to self and rising to Christ on a daily basis, as we open ourselves to the transforming power of the Holy Spirit by placing ourselves in God's hands. I'll come back to what that means in practical terms later.

This then, is the transforming work of the Holy Spirit, helping us day by day, in that powerful Trinitarian image, to place ourselves in God's hands, so that through the death of Jesus on the cross, we can die to self and be raised with Christ and so be transformed by the power of the Holy Spirit.

The refreshing work of the Holy Spirit:
- Firstly, For All
- Secondly, To Transform

3) The Refreshing Work of the Holy Spirit for Mission

'....and began to speak in other languages...'

This was the start of the fulfilment of the prophetic words of the risen Jesus that we find recorded in Acts 1:8, 'But you will receive power when the Holy Spirit has come upon you and you will be my witnesses in Jerusalem, in all Judea and Samaria and to the ends of the earth'.

In the village in which my wife and I lived when we were first married, was an Anglican church with a graveyard. Its claim to fame was a massive rough-hewn granite headstone which stood, perhaps, six feet high in the centre of the graveyard. It marked the burial place of Henry Morton Stanley, the man who travelled to Africa and who, according to popular tradition, said in 1871 those much quoted words 'Dr Livingstone I presume'. This story may be apocryphal, as certainly neither Stanley nor Livingstone recorded those words in that form, but Stanley's gravestone stands as a reminder of a time of missionary activity when people travelled deep into unexplored places such as central Africa with the message of the Gospel. Today, of course, the task of mission and evangelism is once more on our own doorstep, as we find all around us those who have little or no knowledge of the message of the Good News of Jesus.

And just as the refreshing work of the Holy Spirit is *for us all and can transform us all,* so we are *all called to the task of mission. All* of them were filled with the Holy Spirit, and together they *all* began to speak in other languages. Mission is not for the special few, but for us all.

One of the great joys of being Principal at Cliff College is the visitors we get and the interesting people that I meet. Some of those visitors are former students, including those who were students fifty or more years previously, and I am always thrilled to hear their stories when they visit. Other people I meet are representatives of various mission agencies who come to talk to me about their work and how it might link with the work of Cliff. Just a couple of weeks ago, I met Dennis Pethers who heads up Viz-a-Viz and the Rooftop Ministries, and over lunch we talked about evangelism and how many people thought that the task of evangelism was beyond them and that this was something that only specialist Evangelists could do. Dennis told me of how, in his work, he tells people that 'If people think a little better of God because they have met us' then we are actually doing the work of an evangelist, and by that definition being an evangelist is something that *all* of us can do.

Ernest Hemingway, in the introduction to a short story called *The Capital of the World* published in 1936, briefly retells a humorous Spanish folk story about a young man called Paco (a diminutive form of Francisco), and his father who live in a village not far from Madrid. There is an argument between the father and the son, and so the young man decides to leave home. Paco goes to Madrid to make his own way in life, and the father loses contact with him. However, the father never forgets his son and some time later he follows Paco to Madrid to try to find him, despite the fact that the father does not know whether or not Paco is still in the city and indeed the father is unsure even if Paco is still alive. The father takes a room in the Hotel Montana and places an advertisement in the local newspaper. Dear Paco, Meet me at the Hotel Montana at noon on Tuesday. All is forgiven, Papa'. As Tuesday arrives the father waits anxiously, watching the clock in the hotel lobby. As the clock moves to indicate that midday has arrived, the father flings open the doors of the hotel lobby and looks into the square. When the father looks out on the square he sees 800 young men – all called Paco – each of them desperately wanting to be reconciled to their father.

It's a powerful story and it's one that many preachers have used in their sermons and in their writings. It conveys, in a very powerful and visual way, the reason for our evangelism and the purpose of the refreshing work of the Holy Spirit. The reason for our evangelism is not to fill pews, nor to fill roles in the church, but is simply that all people are already loved by God *and not all of them know this yet*. We, who claim to know this wonderful grace of God, are called to share this good news with others in the power of the Holy Spirit. We are to be open to the refreshing work of the Holy Spirit in our lives because this refreshing is *for all*, it is *for transformation* and it is *for mission*.

But as I draw to a close, one question remains. It's a simple and straightforward question. It's the question 'How?'

At the end of his sermon on the day of Pentecost, Peter, emboldened by the outpouring of the Holy Spirit, proclaims the message of Jesus as 'both Lord and Messiah' (v. 36). The crowd respond with a question to Peter and the others which is, at the same time, both simple and profound. It is the question, 'Brothers, what should we do?' Peter's answer is equally simple and profound as he says to the crowd, 'Repent, and be baptised every one of you, in the name of Jesus Christ, so that your sins may be forgiven; and you will receive the gift of the Holy Spirit. For the promise is for you, for your children and for all who are far away, everyone whom the Lord our God calls to him' (v. 38-39).

'What should we do?' ask the crowd. Peter replies by inviting them to pray a prayer of repentance and then to make use of the sign and symbol of baptism that God has provided for them.

We must do the same and begin by putting ourselves in a right relationship with God through our prayers of repentance. Peter is clear that the refreshing gift of the Holy Spirit is for all, and we find this idea repeated several times in his reply to the crowd, but it is clear that the gift of the Holy Spirit comes in the context of a renewed relationship with God which begins with repentance. Speaking personally, my first experience of the refreshing power of the Holy Spirit came at a moment when I was particularly aware of my failure to live in the way of Christian discipleship in that, in a particular context, I was failing to speak up for the values of the Kingdom. At that moment of weakness and repentance, on a very wet evening in a tent in a field at Greenbelt way back in the 1970s, it was, as a friend encouraged me to pray a prayer of repentance and new beginnings, that I felt the deep washing and refreshing power of the Holy Spirit as never before. This prayer, was about no longer trying to please God in my own strength, but instead wanting to live in his strength, and was for me a turning point in my relationship with God and in my new openness to the work of the Holy Spirit.

So the answer to the 'How?' question begins with prayer, but it moves on to action. For the crowd it was the action of baptism. This may still be the action God requires of some today. However, for those of us who have been baptised, the actions will be different and will perhaps involve the discipline of what John Wesley called the 'means of grace', so that, alongside our prayers, we make the commitment to put ourselves in places where God is more able to work in our lives. Of course, God can break into our experience at any time and in any place, but Wesley was clear that those who sought to be more open to the power of the working of God in their lives should be diligent in their commitment to these 'means of grace'. Wesley wrote that a sacrament was not only 'An outward sign of an inward grace' but was also 'a means whereby we receive the same'.

Those phrases come from Wesley's sermon, *The Means of Grace*, and in that sermon he goes on to describe what these 'means of grace' are in more detail:

> The chief of these means are prayer, whether in secret or with the great congregation; searching the scriptures (which implies reading, hearing and meditating thereon); and receiving the Lord's supper, eating bread and drinking wine in remembrance of him: and these we believe to be ordained of God, as the

ordinary channels of conveying his grace to the souls of men.

Wesley then goes on to offer some practical advice, reminding his listeners that, not only is God above all means, but that there is no power in the means themselves. He then challenges them in these words,

> In using all means, seek God alone. In and through every outward thing, look singly to the power of his Spirit and the merits of his Son

'What should we do?' asked the crowd on the day of Pentecost, as they wanted to share in the experience of the refreshing work of the Holy Spirit that they witnessed with their own eyes. Peter's answer to the crowd is also for us. It is the invitation to be open to God through prayer, through engagement with the Scriptures and through the worshipping life of the Church. Wesley's words put it so succinctly and so powerfully, '...seek God alone...look singly to the power of his Spirit and the merits of his Son'.

Conclusion

'All of them were filled with the Holy Spirit and began to speak in other languages, as the Spirit gave them ability'.

Our text from Acts 2:4 speaks of the refreshing work of the Holy Spirit. The Holy Spirit is given to all, and for the transformation of all, so that all might share in mission to the many in this world who have become separated and estranged from their heavenly Father. It is a big task, but Jesus claimed that it was to our advantage that he would go away, for then the Holy Spirit would be sent in a new and more powerful way, and the followers of Jesus – all of us – would be transformed for mission in the Spirit's power.

A closing prayer:

Lord God, we come to you in repentance for the times when we have tried to be followers of Jesus in our own strength. Forgive us, and refresh us, individually and as a Church, with the power of the Holy Spirit, that we might all be transformed in your love and sent out as your missional people in the Spirit's power. In the name of Jesus we pray; Amen.

CONCLUSION
John Wiltshire
Superintendent Minister, Ringsash Circuit

In 2 Timothy 3:16-17, Paul writes, 'All Scripture is God-breathed and is useful for teaching, rebuking, correcting and training in righteousness, so that the man of God may be thoroughly equipped for every good work'. This is very much the mandate for our *Digging for Treasure* Expository Preaching Conferences and the publications that accompany them. I do hope you have found this book to be challenging, encouraging and helpful as we have focussed particularly on Expository Preaching again, this time with specific reference to the theme of Revelation and the sadly neglected, often misunderstood, but powerfully relevant book of the same name. 'All Scripture is useful' - it's up to us to mine out the treasures - and we've been given excellent teaching on how, under the guidance of the Holy Spirit, to do this.

It remains only for me to sum up in conclusion. Being a preacher, I have three points!

Firstly, amongst the multiple instructive and helpful things Steve Brady writes, I am struck by a sentence in his case study of Revelation 12, 'the passage is emphasising the utter oneness and completeness of the ministry of this Child. He is victorious.' How the original readers needed to hear that, and how we need to hear it today. What a vital truth! In his little book on Revelation, Richard Bewes, one of our previous speakers at the conference, quotes from the evangelist Festo Kivengere, former Bishop of Kigezi, Uganda, during the reign of terror of Idi Amin some decades ago:

> Please don't be shocked if you hear that there is revolution in Burundi, Uganda or Zaire. This

> is Africa! It's exciting - as exciting as Europe was three hundred years ago. It's nothing when young countries get revolutions. They are going to get some more. But that does not mean that the man of Galilee has vacated the throne! Christianity has never been scared of a revolution. Satan can roar like a lion, but he has no authority to shake the throne on which Jesus is sitting!

As the Moravians say, 'Our Lamb Conquers'. God is still on the Throne. He is victorious. May we preach in the light of this great truth, come what may.

Secondly Peter Graves and Steve Brady both make 'the biggest point of all' that as we seek to expound the Bible, we must have at the very centre of our hearts and minds what is summed up in the request of the Greeks to Philip in John 12:21, 'Sir ... we would like to see Jesus'. To quote Martin Luther, 'as we go to the cradle only in order to find the baby, so we go to the Scriptures only to find Christ'.

Chris Blake wrote about the Refreshing Work of the Holy Spirit - for all, to transform and in mission. The very centre of the Holy Spirit's gracious and powerful ministry is to shine the spotlight on the Lord Jesus Christ. How we constantly need more of his enabling! 'Our Gospel came to you not simply with words, but also with power, with the Holy Spirit and with deep conviction' (1 Thessalonians 1:5). This needs to be our constant prayer: 'Breathe on us Breath of God'

Thirdly and finally, let me quote some unpublished words of Peter Graves, which further develop his theme, reflecting on Proverbs 29:18, with which it seems fitting to close, 'Without Vision, the people perish'. He wrote:

I knew the verse by heart. It had inspired me, so I wanted to preach on it. To begin my preparation, I looked it up in the NRSV. That presented a problem. It wasn't there. Moving on to the NIV, I still couldn't find it. The NRSV speaks of 'prophecy' without which 'the people cast off restraint.' The NIV bemoans the lack of 'revelation' and warns that the same consequences would follow. But I wanted to talk about the need for vision and not perishing, so I went back to Proverbs 29:18 in the KJV and began to ask why, in later versions the Hebrew had been translated differently. Gradually, I realised that 'Prophecy' refers to the truth that God, through his messengers, wants to share with his people. Similarly, it is through 'Revelation' that God shows what he is like, and how he wants us to live. Both words refer to our catching the 'Vision' of his will and then living accordingly. To obey God's law, leads to our being truly blessed and happy. Disobedience, on the other hand, causes us to ignore the law with its guidelines for responsible living. It causes us to 'cast off restraint', for to go our own self-centred, negative and sinful way will cause us to perish.

Generations of Methodist Ministers have been trained for their life's work at Wesley House in Cambridge. As they stood at the front of the Chapel to lead worship or to preach, they would have looked at the beautiful stained glass window over the entrance. It depicts the New Jerusalem. The vision of eternal life is there before them. The Christian life is a pilgrimage, a journey towards a goal. As preachers we are called to share that vision, to offer Christ, and so encourage our listeners to discover the reality of eternal life for themselves.

To that I can only say 'Amen'!